Someone Who Cares

When you have a sister,
you always have someone
to turn to,
to talk to,
to lean on,
depend on,
to share with,
just be with...
you always have someone
who cares.

THOMAS J. LANGLEY

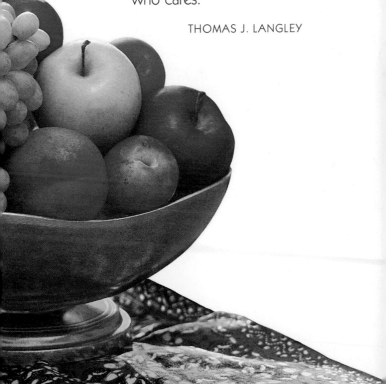

A Sister's Gifts

Her patient understanding
    of the things I do and feel,
the warmth of her encouragement
    and praise,
her close and lasting friendship
    and the pleasure that it brings,
her cheerfulness
    that brightens up my days...
her way of sharing all my hopes,
    the secrets of my heart,
believing in the things
    I'm dreaming of —
these cherished gifts she brings to me
    all help me realize
my sister
    is a special gift of love.

FELICIA WEST

SPEAKING OF SISTERS

Speaking of Sisters

THESE SPECIAL THOUGHTS
REMIND ME OF YOU

Selected by Karen Becraft Rutz

HALLMARK EDITIONS

Acknowledgments:

"Themes and Variations" from SISTERS by Elizabeth Fishel. Copyright © 1979 by Elizabeth Fishel.
Reprinted by permission of William Morrow & Company and The Sterling Lord Agency, Inc.
"Truth Reflected" from AIM FOR A STAR © 1964 by Helen Lowrie Marshall. Reprinted by permission.
© 1980 Hallmark Cards, Inc., Kansas City, Missouri. Printed in the United States of America.

You're loved
        because you're special...
you're special
        because you're you.

She's Your Sister

She's someone who knows
　　every dream you pursue,
　　what you think, how you feel,
　　why you do what you do...
She's someone who knows
　　the real, innermost you
　　and loves who you are...
　　she's your sister.

REBECCA JANE COLEMAN

A
Sister is
a

The strength of family
and the comfort of friendship
are blessings of
a sister's love.

JESSICA RYAN

forever
friend.

Day-Brightener

...when the telephone rings
and brings
at the other end
the warm, loving voice
of my sister...
my friend!

CECIL NELSON

Special Talents

Sisters have a talent
for chasing clouds away,
for painting rainbows
and launching dreams
like kites in an endless sky...
for building sand castles
that don't wash away...
for filling days with laughter
and hearts with loving thoughts...
Sisters have a talent
for caring, for sharing,
for creating warm,
wonderful memories,
for giving life a special
and meaningful touch.

R. A. TANKERSLEY

A Lovely Magic

Sisters work a lovely magic
that turns the blues
into sunny yellows,
Mondays into Fridays,
mistakes into laughter,
and happiness shared
into warmest affection.

STEVE FINKEN

Sisters
add ribbons
and roses

A sister is a source of joy,
a very special part
Of loving memories cherished
forever in the heart.

MARJORIE FRANCES AMES

to everyday bouquets.

Coming Home Again

She knows just where I dream to go,
    remembers where I've been,
Accepts me just the way I am
    and treats me like a friend,
She's someone who is there for me
    no matter what or when,
And every time I'm with her,
    it's like coming home again.

DOROTHY COLGAN

Themes and Variations

The family is a piece of music;
each sister plays
a different theme,
a different variation,
according to her own vision,
tempo, mood,
instrumentation.
No one hears and understands
the echoes,
repetitions,
nuances
and crescendos
as a sister does.

ELIZABETH FISHEL

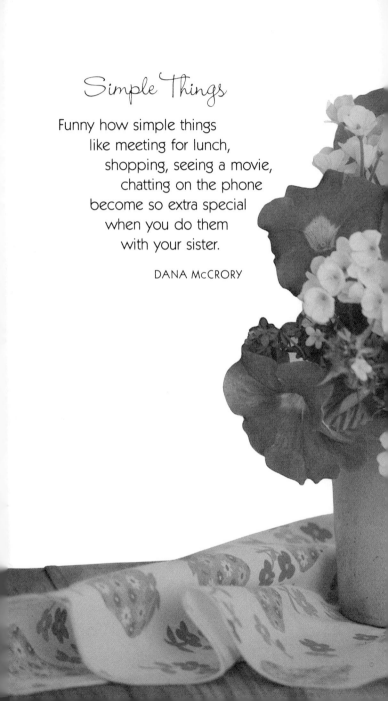

Simple Things

Funny how simple things
like meeting for lunch,
shopping, seeing a movie,
chatting on the phone
become so extra special
when you do them
with your sister.

DANA McCRORY

Sisters

Like branches on a tree,
sisters may grow
in different directions,
yet their roots are one...
each life will always be
a special part of the other.

JUDITH MOORE

Together Time

When the coffee is hot,
and the talk is good,
and the feeling is easy,
and the laughter is light,
and the memories are many,
but the time is too short...
you know you're with
a special "friend"...
your sister.

DEAN WALLEY

A Sister

A sister is someone
    you know you can turn to,
who makes it her special concern
    to be kind,
Someone to count on
    day in and day out
to ease any worry or doubt
    on your mind.
She's someone with praise
    for the good things you've done
and a talent for thinking of fun
    things to do...
A sister is someone
    so nice to be near,
someone you'll love and hold dear
    your life through.

KAREN RAVN

Truth Reflected

You are a mirror
      wherein I see
Myself — as I am,
      and as I should be.
I talk and you listen —
      that's all you do,
And yet I see
      in the eyes of you
The pattern of life
      fall into place —
The truth reflected
      in your face.

HELEN LOWRIE MARSHALL

"Sister"
is a
special

Words that are thoughtful,
smiles that are bright,
deeds that are helpful
and cheering
Always are welcome
and such a delight,
always are
warmly endearing.

ELEANOR LEAH WOODS

*word
for love.*

A sister reaches out
     with understanding
  to warm your world
    and touch your heart
with love.

NORA PARK DANIELS